GEORGE WASHINGTON

The
CROSSING

Written and designed by **Jack E. Levin**

Preface by **Mark R. Levin**

Threshold Editions

NEW YORK LONDON TORONTO SYDNEY NEW DELHI

I dedicate this book to my wife, Norma,
and to my family and all the families
who love the United States of America.

Threshold Editions
A Division of Simon & Schuster, Inc.
1230 Avenue of the Americas
New York, NY 10020

First Threshold Editions hardcover edition June 2013

THRESHOLD EDITIONS and colophon
are trademarks of Simon & Schuster, Inc.

For information about special discounts for bulk purchases, please contact
Simon & Schuster Special Sales at 1-866-506-1949
or business@simonandschuster.com.

The Simon & Schuster Speakers Bureau can bring authors to your live event.
For more information or to book an event, contact the
Simon & Schuster Speakers Bureau at 1-866-248-3049
or visit our website at www.simonspeakers.com.

Manufactured in the United States of America

9   10   8

ISBN 978-1-4767-3193-3
ISBN 978-1-4767-3194-0 (ebook)

PREFACE

This book, *George Washington: The Crossing*, is written and designed by my most important mentor, my father, about one of the greatest statesmen past or present, George Washington, respecting one of the most improbable yet consequential battles in American history, the Battle of Trenton.

My father, Jack, is eighty-eight years old and shows no sign of slowing. He has now authored three books, two in the last two years. His great passion is American history. His knowledge is extensive and he is mostly self-taught. From the earliest days, when our family gathered around the table for breakfast and dinner, my father would introduce various historical facts and events to us, hoping to pique our curiosity about our country. As we grew into teenagers, our discussions would frequently turn into vigorous debates, often requiring moderation from my mother, Norma. Indeed, my brothers—Doug and Rob—and I quickly figured out that we had better do some of our own independent research if we were to have any chance of holding our own at the table. It is from this experience that my brothers and I have acquired a lifelong fascination with the American heritage. Like my father, I cannot digest enough information about those who came before us and built this magnificent nation. There is so much to learn and only one life in which to learn it!

Having written about Abraham Lincoln in *Abraham Lincoln's Gettysburg Address—Illustrated*, my father has now turned his attention to George Washington. There is so much that can be said about Washington. In fact, many books have been written about him. However, my father believes that it is particularly important at this time in our history, when so many of our fellow Americans are anxious if not fearful about the country's future, that he help focus our attention on one of Washington's most remarkable achievements—the American victory at the Battle of Trenton during the Revolutionary War.

On June 15, 1775, the Second Continental Congress elected Washington commander of the nascent Continental Army. According to the *Journals of the Continental Congress:* "The congress met according to adjournment. The president from the chair informed Geo. Washington Esqr. that he had the order of the Congress to acq[ain]t him, that the Congress had by a unanimous vote made choice of him to be general and com[mander] in chief to take the supreme command of the forces raised and to be raised, in defence of American Liberty, and desired his acceptance of it."

Washington responded: "Tho' I am truly sensible of the high Honour done me, in this Appointment, yet I feel great distress, from a consciousness that my abilities and military experience may not be equal to the extensive and important Trust: However, as the Congress desire it, I will enter upon the momentous duty, and exert every power I possess in their service, and for support of the glorious cause. I beg they will accept my most cordial thanks for this distinguished testimony of their approbation. But, lest some unlucky event should happen, unfavourable to my reputation, I beg it may be remembered, by every Gentleman in the room, that I, this day, declare with the utmost sincerity, I do not think myself equal to the Command I am honored with."

Just as Washington would later reluctantly attend the Constitutional Convention in 1787 and then preside over it, and humbly accept the unanimous election by electoral college as the first president of the United States, Washington reluctantly and humbly accepted the assignment of commander of the Continental Army. He would become the most beloved man in America.

Before the Battle of Trenton, the Continental Army had lost battles in New York and retreated through New Jersey to Pennsylvania. The Revolutionary War seemed lost. But the army's remarkable victory at the Battle of Trenton on December 26, 1776, under Washington's brilliant leadership, would change the course of the war and, more broadly, history forever.

As this book, *George Washington: The Crossing*, attests, my father has a truly unique ability to let history speak for itself through his careful use of prose and painstaking selection of illustrations and photographs. There is fresh simplicity yet bracing depth in every page of this book. And unlike too many authors, my father is not interested in exploiting the human imperfections and frailties of the Founders but, instead, presents a straightforward account of these mostly selfless, heroic American figures, who were willing to die for the cause of freedom and self-government, and among whom Washington was arguably the most significant.

There is much to appreciate and celebrate about our American legacy, and there is no better man to remind us of our great blessings than my father, Jack E. Levin, a true patriot.

—Mark R. Levin

After the Battle of Trenton, members of the Continental Congress, interested in how his troops responded to offensive action after a year of defeat and retreat from the enemy, wrote Washington asking how his troops performed during the battle. General Washington's letter written in response to the president of the Continental Congress, John Hancock, on December 27, 1776, is printed in this book in RED lettering. These are Washington's own words, enhanced with contemporary drawings of the time, telling his story of the Battle of Trenton.

"May I be pardoned if, upon this occasion, I mention that away back in my childhood, the earliest days of my being able to read, I got hold of a small book, such a one as few of the younger members have ever seen—Weems' 'Life of Washington.' I remember all the accounts there given of the battlefields and struggles for the liberties of the country, and none fixed themselves upon my imagination so deeply as the struggle here at Trenton, New Jersey. The crossing of the river, the contest with the Hessians, the great hardships endured at the time, all fixed themselves on my memory more than any single revolutionary event; and you all know, for you all have been boys, how these early impressions last longer than any others. I recollect thinking then, boy even though I was, that there must have been something more than common that those men struggled for."

—Abraham Lincoln addressing the Senate
of the State of New Jersey, 1861

FOREWORD

During the second week of March 1776, General George Washington scored a major victory four months before the Declaration of Independence was signed. He forced the British to leave the city of Boston, where the spark of the Revolution had been struck.

Washington had the heavy cannons that Colonel Henry Knox and his men had valiantly brought from Fort Ticonderoga and placed into position on Dorchester Heights, a piece of hilly land projecting into Boston Harbor. He had fortified the two highest hills, Bunker and Breed's hills, and bombarded Boston and Boston Harbor with deadly shellfire daily.

The constant American bombardment convinced General Lord William Howe, commander of the British army in Boston, that only an evacuation of the city would save his troops from a military disaster.

In the following days Howe loaded 9,000 soldiers and their supplies on nearly 100 ships and sailed away, apparently headed for Halifax, Nova Scotia.

The remaining Boston residents wildly hailed the American victory, but Washington did not take part. Instead he stared out to sea, wondering about the real destination of Lord Howe and the Royal Navy.

General Washington could not believe Howe was really en route to Halifax. With all the troops, ships, and war material the British had at their command, a movement to Nova Scotia would be a foolish mistake. It seemed to him a more realistic possibility that Howe might risk an attempt to take New York City and its great seaport.

The loss of New York City would be a terrible setback for the Americans. To check such a potential British manuver, Washington rushed troops overland from Boston to New York City. He set his men digging entrenchments from the Battery to the northern tip of Manhattan Island.

Washington had guessed right. Late in June 1776 the missing British fleet appeared. Lord Howe had more than 100 ships loaded with thousands of British and Hessian troops for an attack on New York City.

And so our story begins. . . .

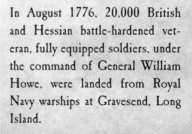

In August 1776, 20,000 British and Hessian battle-hardened veteran, fully equipped soldiers, under the command of General William Howe, were landed from Royal Navy warships at Gravesend, Long Island.

Royal Navy ships land Howe's army of British and Hessian troops.

They attacked and smashed through the American Force stationed on Long Island by Washington to repel any attempt by the British to take New York City. Before the overwhelming English assault, the Colonial army was forced to fall back.

The Continental Army on Long Island retreats from the British and Hessian army's overpowering attack.

General William Howe.

A valiant rearguard delaying action by Delaware and Maryland Continentals, commanded by General William Alexander, Lord Stirling, allowed the retreating Americans enough time to safely reach General Washington's entrenchments at Brooklyn Heights.

General William Alexander, Lord Stirling.
Lord Stirling leading his brave troops in battle
against the British and Hessians at Long Island.

The British continued their assault on the Americans. With his back to open water and outnumbered, Washington was in danger of losing his whole army. He ordered his men to gather all the boats they could find and bring them to the East River at dusk. Colonel John Glover's regiment of Massachusetts fishermen began the enormous task of transporting the American troops at night in a rainstorm to Manhattan Island. It was done so quietly the enemy never knew it was happening. The Americans got away with all their guns, horses, food, and ammunition. Washington took one of the last boats to cross as the foggy dawn lifted, and Howe and the Redcoats found Brooklyn empty.

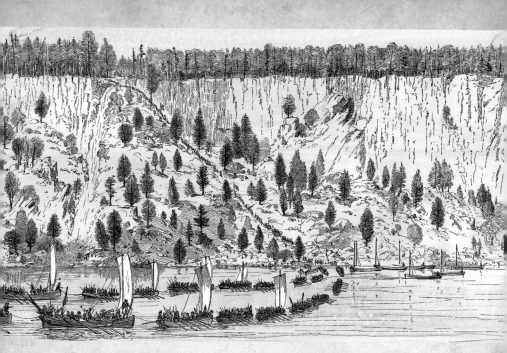

British troops climb the Jersey Palisades to successfully attack and seize Fort Lee.

The British pressed their assault on the Americans, forcing General Washington to retreat from his positions in Manhattan, leaving Fort Washington, on the New York shore, and Fort Lee, on the New Jersey side of the Hudson River, to defend themselves against the entire British army and navy. The two forts fell to the Redcoats in quick succession with the loss of large quantities of valuable supplies and 2,600 American officers and men taken prisoners.

facing page: Map showing the area of General Washington's retreat through Long Island, Manhattan, and New Jersey.

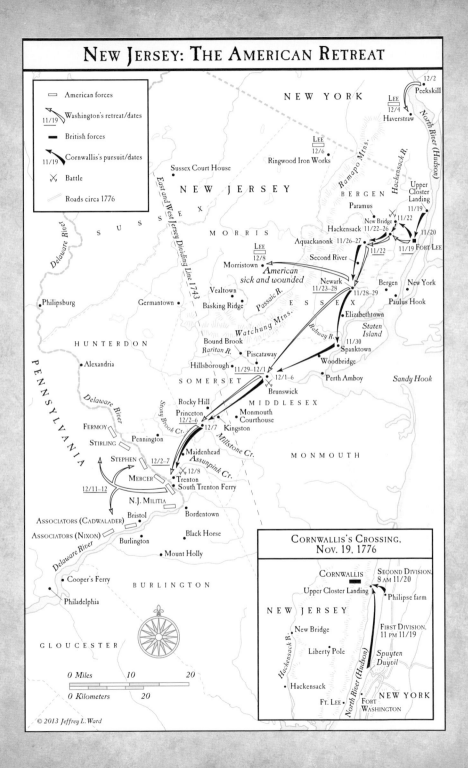

NEW JERSEY: THE AMERICAN RETREAT

Legend:
- American forces
- 11/19 Washington's retreat/dates
- British forces
- 11/19 Cornwallis's pursuit/dates
- ✕ Battle
- Roads circa 1776

NEW YORK

12/2 Peekskill
LEE 12/4 Haverstraw
LEE 12/6 Ringwood Iron Works

Sussex Court House

NEW JERSEY

BERGEN
Paramus 11/19
Hackensack 11/22-26
New Bridge 11/22
Aquackanonk 11/26-27
11/22
Second River
11/20
11/19 FORT LEE

Upper Closter Landing

North River (Hudson)

Ramapo Mtns.

Hackensack R.

Delaware River

S U S S E X

East and West Jersey Dividing Line 1743

M O R R I S

LEE 12/8
Morristown

American sick and wounded

Vealtown
Germantown
Basking Ridge

Philipsburg

Passaic R.

Newark 11/23-28
11/28-29

Bergen   New York
Paulus Hook

Elizabethtown

E S S E X

Watchung Mtns.

Staten Island

H U N T E R D O N

Bound Brook
Raritan R.   Piscataway
Hillsborough
11/29-12/1

Rahway R.

11/30 Spanktown
Woodbridge

Alexandria

S O M E R S E T

12/1-6
Brunswick

Perth Amboy   Sandy Hook

Delaware River

Strong Brook Cr.

Rocky Hill
Princeton 12/2-6
12/7 Kingston

M I D D L E S E X

Monmouth Courthouse

Millstone Cr.

M O N M O U T H

P E N N S Y L V A N I A

FERMOY
STIRLING
Pennington
STEPHEN   12/2-7
Maidenhead
Assunpink Cr.
MERCER   ✕ 12/8
Trenton
South Trenton Ferry

12/11-12

N.J. MILITIA

ASSOCIATORS (CADWALADER)
ASSOCIATORS (NIXON)
Bristol
Burlington
Bordentown
Black Horse
Mount Holly

Cooper's Ferry

B U R L I N G T O N

Philadelphia

G L O U C E S T E R

0 Miles   10   20
0 Kilometers   20

CORNWALLIS'S CROSSING, NOV. 19, 1776

CORNWALLIS   SECOND DIVISION, 8 AM 11/20
Upper Closter Landing   Philipse farm

NEW JERSEY

Hackensack R.
New Bridge
Liberty Pole
Hackensack

FIRST DIVISION, 11 PM 11/19
Spuyten Duyvil

North River (Hudson)

Ft. Lee   FORT WASHINGTON

NEW YORK

© 2013 Jeffrey L. Ward

Having lost Long Island, Brooklyn, and Manhattan to the enemy, Washington realized General Howe's next target would be the capital of the Revolution, the city of Philadelphia, Pennsylvania. His plan called for reaching Pennsylvania before the British.

On November 12, 1776, Washington led 3,000 men across the Hudson River into New Jersey. General Lord Cornwallis, commanding 10,000 British and Hessian troops, quickly followed, confident they'd catch and destroy the Americans in a short time. Pursuing the rebels relentlessly, they did not allow them to rest.

General Washington and his army retreating across New Jersey.

The weather turned cold and a steady chilling rain fell heavily. Weary, disheartened, sick, poorly equipped, with losses from death and desertion growing daily, Washington's little army retreated westward across New Jersey. A pursuing British officer wrote, "Many of the Rebels who were killed were without shoes and stockings, and several were observed to have only linen drawers, also in great want of blankets, they must suffer extremely." They did. But still they struggled onward.

Charles Cornwallis, British general, on November 25, 1776, set off across New Jersey with 10,000 men, determined to catch Washington, he said, as a hunter bags a fox.

Barely keeping his exhausted army ahead of the onrushing British, Washington reached the Delaware River on December 8, 1776. He ordered his troops to seize and destroy all the available boats in the area, except those he needed, then they crossed into Pennsylvania.

With the river between his troops and the British army, Washington halted the retreat and turned his tired, ragged army to face the enemy. Utterly exhausted, freezing, and starved, they awaited the next move by the Redcoats. It started to snow . . . large pieces of ice began to form and float downstream. Fortunately for the Americans, General Howe decided his army would not take the field in the dead of winter. Why bother? According to all reports there would be no rebel army left to face his men come spring.

As 1776, a year of terrible suffering and humiliating defeats, drew to a close, the American cause seemed doomed. The Revolution was crumbling.

Washington's troops encamped along the Delaware River in 1776.
They suffered greatly from lack of winter clothing, food, and shelter.

Thomas Paine, an Englishman who came to America because
he believed the colonists' revolt against English rule to be right.

Thomas Paine, the author of the very popular pamphlet *Common
Sense*, joined Washington's army as a volunteer. During the retreat
across New Jersey he wrote a very powerful essay, "The American
Crisis." It impressed Washington so much he ordered it read before
each regiment.

The *American* CRISIS.

NUMBER I.

By the Author of COMMON SENSE.

THESE are the times that try men's souls: The summer soldier and the sunshine patriot will, in this crisis, shrink from the service of his country; but he that stands it NOW, deserves the love and thanks of man and woman. Tyranny, like hell, is not easily conquered; yet we have this consolation with us, that the harder the conflict, the more glorious the triumph. What we obtain too cheap, we esteem too lightly:—'Tis dearness only that gives every thing its value. Heaven knows how to set a proper price upon its goods; and it would be strange, indeed, if so celestial an article as FREEDOM should not be highly rated. Britain, with an army to enforce her tyranny, has declared, that she has a right (*not only to* TAX, but) "to "BIND *us in* ALL CASES WHATSOEVER," and if being *bound in that manner* is not slavery, then is there not such a thing as slavery upon earth. Even the expression is impious, for so unlimited a power can belong only to GOD.

WHETHER the Independence of the Continent was declared too soon, or delayed too long, I will not now enter into as an argument; my own simple opinion is, that had it been eight months earlier, it would have been much better. We did not make a proper use of last winter, neither could we, while we were in a dependent state. However, the fault, if it were one, was all our own; we have none to blame but ourselves*. But no great deal is lost yet; all that Howe has been doing for this month past is rather a ravage than a conquest, which the spirit of the Jersies a year ago would have quickly repulsed, and which time and a little resolution will soon recover.

I have as little superstition in me as any man living, but my

*"The present winter" (meaning the last) " is worth an " age if rightly employed, but if lost, or neglected, the whole " Continent will partake of the evil; and there is no punish- " ment that man does not deserve, be he who, or what, or " where he will, that may be the means of sacrificing a season " so precious and useful." COMMON SENSE.

It began: "These are the times that try men's souls: The summer soldier and the sunshine patriot will, in the crisis, shrink from the service of his country; but he that stands it now, deserves the love and thanks of man and woman. Tyranny, like hell, is not easily conquered; yet we have this consolation with us, that the harder the conflict, the more glorious the triumph."

Washington sadly wrote to his brother John, "I think the game is pretty near up. . . . You can form no idea of the perplexity of my situation. No man, I believe, ever had a greater choice of difficulties and less means to extricate himself from them."

General George Washington, commander in chief of the Continental Army.

Washington and his exhausted army were encamped on the Pennsylvania side of the Delaware River at a place called McKonkey's Ferry. At Trenton, on the New Jersey side of the river about nine miles downstream, was Colonel Johann Rall with 1,400 battle-hardened professional Hessian soldiers. Washington pondered over his maps and plans in his headquarters. He looked out on the river with its floating blocks of ice, and the snow-covered hills, and his desolated men gathered around campfires freezing and hungry. He had to do something. The terms of militia enlistments would run out on New Year's Day, and many of his troops would leave with it. It was late December. He had only a few days open to him. He called his staff together for a council of war to outline his plans. He would take his little army across the river and attack Trenton. The officers were enthusiastic about his plan and decided to cross into New Jersey late on Christmas night when they knew the Hessians would be celebrating and least likely to expect any action by the Americans. So very determined to succeed at their task were these men that the passwords "VICTORY OR DEATH" were chosen for the attack.

"The evening of the 25th I ordered the troops to parade in back of McKonkey's Ferry, that they might begin to pass as soon as it grew dark, imagining we should be able to throw all over, with the necessary artillary, by 12 o'clock, and easily arrive at Trenton by five in the morning, the distance being about nine miles.

Late in the afternoon on Christmas day the Colonial troops were ordered to move. They made their way down to the riverbank, where, in shivering silence, they started loading the boats. Fifty big artillery horses balked at being led onto the boats. They snorted and stamped on the ground with their hooves, rearing up because they were very nervous. Eighteen cannons, weighing a few hundred pounds each, had to be loaded and tied down so they wouldn't move once the boats started their journey across the ice-choked river. If a horse made a violent movement or a cannon broke loose from its mooring, the boat, which was overcrowded with troops, would capsize and all on board would perish because of the freezing water.

Colonel Knox had charge of loading the boats. It was a slow, cold job lasting until three o'clock in the morning. Finally they got under way. It was pitch dark. Complete silence was called for. Only the sound of the oars pushing the water and the ice cakes bumping the sides of the boats could be heard. There was no talking or cursing or smoking allowed.

But the quantity of ice made that night

The Delaware River on Christmas night 1776 was a torrent of rushing water blocked with large pieces of ice. The weather was extremely cold, with a biting wind and a driving sleet storm covering everything with a coating of ice. The Hessians, upon viewing the condition of the river, could not imagine anyone daring to cross it on a night such as this. They retired to their quarters to partake in hot meals and drink rum.

Ice floes on the Delaware River.

Things were different on the Pennsylvania side of the river. Washington ordered all of the "Durham" boats that had been seized and hidden away brought out to the embarkation point. These boats were like oversized canoes, sixty feet long, eight feet wide, shallow draft, pointed at both ends. They were very hard vessels to navigate under the best of conditions, and a perilous means of conveyance for troops and their equipment in the dreadful weather of that night.

A Durham boat

*impeded the passage of the boats so much that it was three
o'clock before the troops took up their line of march*

Colonel Henry Knox, artillery commander of the American army,
wrote of the crossing in a letter to his wife on December 28, 1776:
"The floating ice on the river made the labor almost incredible. However, perseverance accomplished what at first seemed impossible.
About four o'clock the troops were all on the Jersey side."

To handle the boats in the crossing of the Delaware, Washington once again called on the reliable Colonel John Glover and his regiment of hardy fishermen from Marblehead, New England. These were the same men who had prevented the retreating American army from being destroyed by the British when they ferried the entire Colonial force of 9,000 men, artillery, horses, and heavy equipment aboard flatboats across the East River at night without the British forces' hearing a thing.

but as I was certain there was no making a retreat without being discovered, and harassed on repassing the river,

---

Already three hours behind schedule, with nine miles yet to cover over ice-glazed roads, Washington still waited at the landing point until all his men, artillery, horses, and equipment were safely ashore.

Then Washington assembled his troops and began the march to Trenton.

Washington watches as all his men, horses, and equipment are safely landed.

I determined to push on....

An American officer wrote. "It will be a terrible night for the men who have no shoes. Some of them have tied old rags around their feet; others are barefoot, but I have not heard a man complain." It was said you could follow the trail of the Colonial soldiers' march toward Trenton by the blood from their bleeding feet on the snow and ice.

inset: Colonel John Glover. Glover's Marblehead men ferrying the American army across the Delaware River into New Jersey.

This made me dispair of surprising the town, as I well knew we could not reach it before the day was fairly broke,

December 26 dawned peaceful and quiet in the little town of Trenton. The Hessian soldiers and their commander, Colonel Johann Rall, had celebrated Christmas by drinking rum and dancing with the town ladies until early predawn hours and now they slept soundly.

A view of the Trenton battlefield as it looked in 1776.

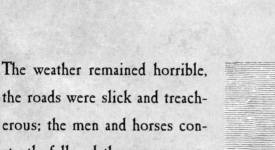

General Nathanial Greene, commander of the American troops that approached Trenton on Pennington Road.

The weather remained horrible, the roads were slick and treacherous; the men and horses constantly fell and the cannon were almost impossible to move.

Halfway to Trenton, Washington ordered his army to split in two. One half, under General John Sullivan, was to proceed on the lower River Road, the other half, commanded by General Nathaniel Greene, was to take the upper Pennington Road. Sullivan reported the rain had soaked his troops' muskets. Washington ordered General Sullivan to tell his men to use their bayonets. He was resolved to take Trenton.

I formed my detachment into two divisions, one to march by the lower or River Road, the other, by the upper or Pennington Road. As the divisions had nearly the same march, I ordered each of them, immediately upon forcing the out guards to push directly into town, that they might charge the enemy before they had time to form.

The upper division arrived at the enemy's advance post exactly at eight o'clock, and in three minutes after I found from the fire on the lower road that that division had also got up.

The out guards made but small opposition, though their numbers were small, they behaved very well keeping up a constant fire from behind houses.

At 7:30 a.m. the Americans rapidly approached the outskirts of Trenton. Suddenly an American advance guard ran into a Hessian picket on Pennington Road. Upon seeing the advancing Colonials, he turned and ran for the town shouting, *"Der Feind! Heraus! Heraus!"* (The enemy! Get up! Get up!)

But it was too late. Musket shots from Sullivan's division signaled their attack at the lower end of town and Washington was leading Greene's division as they ran into the upper end of town shooting and shouting their passwords as they ran toward the Hessian enemy; "Victory or Death!"

The Hessians try to form up and battle the Americans but they fail against the Colonials' onslaught.

We presently saw their main body formed, but from their motions, they seemed undetermined how to act.

The Hessians were slow in rousing after their festive Christmas evening. They rushed into the streets, but still in a daze from their partying, they staggered and tumbled over one another, falling in the wet snow and mud. The Hessians were unable to form ranks.

Colonel Rall was awakened from his drunken sleep by the shouting of his men and the American cannons and musket fire. He unsteadily rushed into the street. He was helped on his horse and, waving his sword, shouted, *"Vorwärts! Vorwärts!"* (Forward! Forward!) His men formed once and tried to charge into the town.

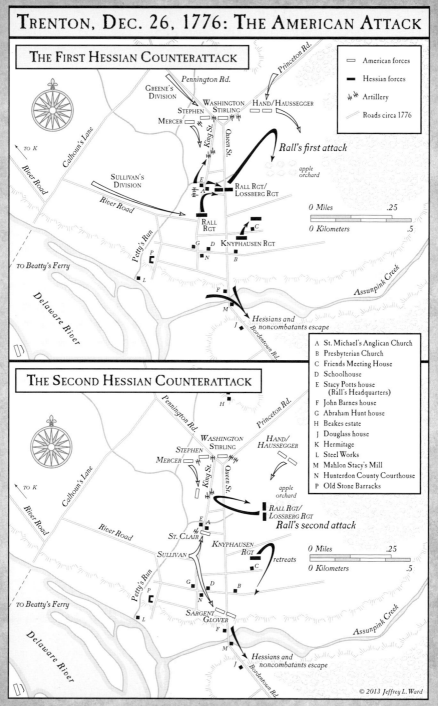

TRENTON, DEC. 26, 1776: THE AMERICAN ATTACK

THE FIRST HESSIAN COUNTERATTACK

Pennington Rd.

Princeton Rd.

GREENE'S DIVISION

WASHINGTON HAND/HAUSSEGGER
STEPHEN STIRLING
MERCER

TO K

Calhoun's Lane

SULLIVAN'S DIVISION

River Road

River Road

Petty's Run

TO Beatty's Ferry

Delaware River

King St.

Queen St.

Rall's first attack

apple orchard

E
A
RALL RGT/
LOSSBERG RGT

RALL RGT

C

G
D
KNYPHAUSEN RGT

P
N
B

L

F

M

Hessians and noncombatants escape

Bordentown Rd.

Assunpink Creek

Legend:
- American forces
- Hessian forces
- ╫╫ Artillery
- Roads circa 1776

0 Miles .25
0 Kilometers .5

THE SECOND HESSIAN COUNTERATTACK

Pennington Rd.

Princeton Rd.

H

WASHINGTON HAND/
STEPHEN STIRLING HAUSSEGGER
MERCER

TO K

Calhoun's Lane

River Road

River Road

Petty's Run

TO Beatty's Ferry

Delaware River

King St.

Queen St.

apple orchard

E
A
ST. CLAIR

SULLIVAN

P
N

L

RALL RGT/
LOSSBERG RGT

Rall's second attack

KNYPHAUSEN RGT

C
retreats

G
D
B

SARGENT
GLOVER

F

M

Hessians and noncombatants escape

Bordentown Rd.

Assunpink Creek

0 Miles .25
0 Kilometers .5

A St. Michael's Anglican Church
B Presbyterian Church
C Friends Meeting House
D Schoolhouse
E Stacy Potts house
   (Rall's Headquarters)
F John Barnes house
G Abraham Hunt house
H Beakes estate
J Douglass house
K Hermitage
L Steel Works
M Mahlon Stacy's Mill
N Hunterdon County Courthouse
P Old Stone Barracks

© 2013 Jeffrey L. Ward

Being hard pressed by our troops, who had already got possession of part of their artillery, they attempted to file off by a road on their right leading to Princeton, but perceiving their intention I threw a body of troops their way which immediately checked them.

But Colonel Knox rolled his cannons into position and swept the streets with artillery fire. The Hessians were mowed down like wheat.

Finding from our disposition that they were surrounded, and that they must inevitably be cut to pieces if they made any further resistance, they agreed to lay down their arms.

When Rall himself was shot down, mortally wounded, the demoralized Hessians' resistance ended and they threw down their arms in surrender.

Colonel Johann Rall is shot from his horse during an effort to beat back the Americans' charge.

The number that submitted in this manner was 23 Officers and 886 men . . . our loss is very trifling, indeed, only two officers and two privates wounded.

Colonel Rall, seriously wounded, is held up by his officers as he surrenders his sword and his army to General Washington.

General John Sullivan,
commander of the southern section of
Washington's army that attacked
Trenton from River Road.

General Henry Knox,
artillery commander for
Washington's army.

Two hundred Hessians escaped and fled. The Americans took 886 officers and men prisoners of war. Another 106 Hessians were killed or wounded. Washington asked for a list of his casualties and was told four men wounded, two officers and two privates.

A fantastic victory indeed.

In justice to the officers and men, I must add that their behavior upon this occasion reflects the highest honor upon them. The difficulty of passing the river on a very severe night, and their marching through a violent storm of snow and hail did in the least abate their ardor. But when they came to charge, each seemed to vie with the other in pressing forward, and were I to give preference to any particular corps, I should do great injustice to the others."

General George Washington

The victory at Trenton lifted the spirits of the patriots. Fatigued, hungry, discouraged, American soldiers who had been on the verge of going home when their enlistment time was up at the end of the year decided to reenlist. Young men from the countryside, stirred up by the Americans' being able to defeat the vaunted Hessian soldiers in battle, came into camp and enlisted. The colonies, when they heard of the Trenton victory, became full of newfound patriotism.

The Congress, who had fled to Baltimore a few days before Christmas, returned to Philadelphia, defiant of the menacing British. The victory at Trenton turned everything around. Washington had shown a capacity of generalship, his ragtag army had shown a willingness to fight and win, his faith in his troops had been justified, his hopes of winning the war were invigorated and . . .

THE AMERICAN REVOLUTION WAS NOT GOING TO COLLAPSE.

facing page: Washington Receiving a Salute on the Field of Trenton, from the engraving by William Holl (1865), after the painting by John Faed.

AUTHOR'S NOTE

The victory at Trenton came as a complete surprise to people and governments all over the world. They could not understand how a ragged, half-frozen, starving assortment of hardly trained civilian troops, on one of the bleakest nights of a bleak year, 1776, of the struggle for independence, could defeat one of the world's best professional armies.

This book is an attempt to explain how and why this effort succeeded. There emerges a picture of the American soldier as a more strongly committed fighter for his cause of freedom and liberty than the professional Hessian soldier whose only interest was the booty victory brought.

The story of the Battle of Trenton certainly demonstrates how highly valued were the rights the revolutionists sought to establish and serves as a reminder that the ideals they so valiantly struggled for are worthy of fighting for today—life, liberty, freedom, and the pursuit of happiness.

—Jack E. Levin

PHOTO CREDITS